Hit  Down
Dammit!

The concept and technique of hitting down
at the golf ball for improved ball striking,
accuracy, distance, and backspin.

Clive Scarff

"Hit Down Dammit!" written and produced by Clive Scarff
Published by Thornhill Press

Photos by Idora Scott
Director of Photography Dave Sanders
Studio: Open Studios, Vancouver BC.
Production Assistant Jamii Coutts
Special Thanks to Chris Hood

ISBN-13: 978-1497406650
ISBN-10: 149740665X

Visit www.hitdowndammit.com
www.clivescarff.com

Contents Dammit!

Author's Introduction

Welcome to *Hit Down Dammit!* What you are about to learn is not new. It is effectively the central ingredient of the golf swing and has been since before the hickory shaft. However, for reasons we can only guess, this key ingredient seems to have become one of the game's biggest secrets.

It shouldn't be.

The secret is simple. In order to hit a good golf shot you must hit down at the ball. You will soon see why, without a clear knowledge and understanding of this principle, almost any other worthwhile instruction or swing theory is rendered useless. And, why even endless hours of practice yield ineffective results.

You will see how a proper understanding of hitting down makes all worthwhile instruction begin to make far more sense, and become much easier to execute, and to memorize. As well, you will see that with this understanding it becomes much easier to weed out the misleading, hackneyed, old clichés of golf instruction that over 500 years after the game's inception continue to permeate throughout the golf world, and stymie even the most dedicated students of the game.

So, open your mind, grab a club, and join me as we learn to *Hit Down Dammit!*

Chapter 1

Golf Is a Difficult Game

 Golf is a difficult game. Yet to so many of the uninitiated it might seem very simple. The objective is to strike a ball... that is just sitting there. How tough can it be?

It's not like baseball, or tennis, where the ball is moving as we attempt to make contact with it. It's not like hockey where someone is trying to knock you down, and if it is, rethinking your choice of foursome should perhaps be the bigger priority. Why is it then, in golf, that this stationary balls so difficult to hit? Why do we miss it completely at times?

Hit Down Dammit!

Golf is difficult, deceptively so, due to our perception of how to get the ball airborne. We want the ball to go up, and our natural inclination is to hit up at it. However, we need to hit down. Part of this initial deception lies in the fact the ball is round, and our clubface is lofted (angled back). On first look it might appear that our goal is to slide the lofted clubhead under the ball, striking its lower half on the upswing, and thus driving - or lifting - the ball into the air. However, it is critical to note that the golf club has not been designed to get under the ball to lift it. It has been designed to strike the ball as the clubhead is descending, on the downswing.

The face of the club will contact the surface of the golf ball just prior to reaching the bottom of the swing arc. As a result, the ball becomes trapped between the descending clubface and the ground. The ball compresses. Because the face of the clubhead is lofted, the ball will - rather than be driven into the ground as a downward hit might imply - spin backwards up the clubface, decompress (adding energy to its escape) and climb into the air. The angle at which the ball climbs (trajectory) will be directly related to the loft of the club we have chosen for the shot.

Unfortunately, until the technicalities of hitting down are fully explained, hitting up seems, on the surface, more logical. If we want something to go up, we tend to hit up at it. If I gave you a tennis ball and a racket, and asked you to hit the ball up into the air, what would you do? You would lower your racket and strike

 up at the tennis ball. And the tennis ball would go up. It's logical. So why wouldn't it be logical in golf too? Certainly – on the surface anyway - hitting *down* at something you want to go up does not appear to be logical.

While the hitting up approach might appear to be more logical, let's look at the downside of such a strategy as it relates to the golf swing.

Figure 1 Despite appearances, the club has not been designed to get under the ball. It's easy to get under the ball in tennis... not so much in golf.

Chapter 2

The Downside of Hitting Up

Hitting up requires striking the lower half of a small object that is situated below you. The portion of the ball we are aiming for is usually sitting on the ground. In grass. All too often, long grass. So, if attempting to hit up at the ball, here is your first question:

Do you want to:

Hit the ground before hitting the ball?

or...

Miss the ground altogether?

2.1 Hitting the Ground Before The Ball

Hitting the ground before the ball (hitting "fat") has a couple of significant negative physical effects, as well as corresponding negative mental effects.

First, hitting the ground prior to hitting the ball will significantly slow the clubhead down. It is worth noting: **clubhead speed is directly related to distance**. Anything we do that causes the clubhead to slow down will unavoidably cost us in terms of distance.

CLUBHEAD SPEED = DISTANCE

Second, hitting the ground prematurely will also alter the angle of the clubface at impact, minimizing any chance of it returning to square to produce a straight shot.

Contact with the golf ball after bottoming out (hitting the ground) means the club will be rising at impact. This makes it very unlikely you will be able to hit the lower half of the ball.

Figure 2   Trying to hit up is the leading cause of hitting the ground before the ball.

Indeed it is far more likely you will strike the mid portion or upper half of the ball with:

Hit Down Dammit!

The leading edge of arising clubface

or:

The sole of the rising clubhead...

Resulting in...

A skulled shot

or:

A topped shot.

Figure 3 After hitting the ground, often the leading edge of the clubhead strikes the upper half of the golf ball as the head is rising, resulting in a 'topped' shot.

Finally, hitting the ground before the ball also... plain old don't feel good! So, what happens after a series of fat shots is we begin to take on the belief that hitting the ground - at all - is not very productive. Now what do we do? Well, naturally (unfortunately) we begin trying to hit up at the ball without hitting the ground.

2.2 Avoiding Hitting the Ground

So you have decided you do not like hitting the ground. Want to avoid it altogether. Well, avoiding hitting the ground yields even further difficulty. This is because we are now trying to hit up... at the lower half of a ball - that is sitting on the ground - without hitting the ground. Imagine the immense talent, skill, and accuracy required to properly time a swing so that the clubhead reaches the bottom of its arc, without hitting the ground, and then - *on the way up* - the face is able to cleanly strike the lower half of a ball that stands 1.5 inches high and is quite likely nestled down in the grass. No wonder we like practicing with a tee! And what is the most likely result of such an effort? Assuming we actually do avoid hitting the ground, we are likely to:

• Have the leading edge of the clubhead strike the middle of the ball and produce a "skull" - a low worm-burning shot that leaves our fingers numb;

• Have the bottom of the club (sole), on its ascent, catch the top of the ball and thus top the ball;

• Miss the ball altogether.

There is a small chance that in attempting to hit up - with rare and fortunate timing - you do manage to avoid the ground and yet make contact with the ball below its equator. At best this is a one in ten chance. The problem is, when we do achieve this we tend to pat ourselves on the back and say," Finally, I got it!" We then proceed to the next shot thinking we have the golf swing solved, not realizing we'd just had a lucky roll of the dice. And worse, still of the illusion that hitting up is what we are supposed to do. Next shot? Well, let's just say there is a nine out of ten chance it won't be good.

Figure 4   *Club has not released, not rotated, has risen too high too soon. This clubface is not square, it is open, relative to where it should be at this point in the swing.*

Aside from the low odds of a successful hit up, it is worth noting that even a successful hit up will never be as good as a mediocre hit down. Why? First, let's go back to the idea of clubhead speed as it relates to distance.

The faster the clubhead is moving at impact, the further the ball will go.

When is the clubhead moving the fastest?

<u>On its way down.</u>

Should you be so lucky as to make clean contact with the ball on the upswing, you will be doing so as the clubhead is slowing down. It is somewhat ironic to think of the effort we make to create speed in the golf swing, only to make contact with the ball as the clubhead is decelerating.

Second, an attempt to hit up will cause the clubhead to deviate from its natural swing path, preventing its rotation back to square at impact. Therefore, if and when we do hit up "successfully", the result will tend to be a weak shot, prone to leaking - or even shooting - directly to the right. Sound familiar?

Thirdly, the ball should rise at an angle that directly relates to the angle of the clubface. This is assuming we are hitting down, and the ball is spinning (backwards) up the clubface. If we are hitting up, this does not happen. The significance of loft is greatly reduced. We are now striking upwards at the ball with a relatively flat piece of metal. The ball will then tend to rise at the angle we are thrusting, rather than the angle of the clubface. **This creates a scenario wherein it seems all our shots are going the same distance, regardless of the club used.** Perhaps this too, sounds familiar?

2.3 Failure to Shift Your Weight

Figure 5   Weight is hanging back in order to hit up.

Another distinct negative associated with hitting up lies in relation to your weight shift. At address, your weight should be evenly distributed, with approximately 50% of your weight on each foot. As you swing back... two arms, your torso, and the club itself move to the right. Thus, quite naturally, your weight shifts to the back (right) foot. As you swing down, the torso, arms, and club move back to the centre and so again, your weight naturally shifts forward to the front foot.

Throw a ball, and note how naturally your weight shifts back, and then forward, toward your target. However, if you are trying to hit up at a golf ball, you simply won't want your weight to shift forward. It is very difficult to hit up and shift your weight forward at the same time. Try it. Instinctively you will want to remain on your back foot in order to slide the club under the ball and thrust upwards. So, if you are attempting to shift your weight forward while at the same time you are of the mindset to hit up, your name is Houston. And Houston, we have a problem. Something will have to give as the two ideas are completely counterproductive. Often the net result will be a back-foot, upward swipe at the ball, followed by a last-second weight shift (after the ball is gone) to satisfy those who told you to shift your weight. This is otherwise known as shutting the gate after the horse has bolted. And very confusing, even to an observer, as your seemingly correct finish position will contribute to the illusion that you shifted your weight properly. This failure to shift your weight - by necessity - will cost you in terms of clubhead speed. That means... distance.

Chapter 3

How Do You Hit Down, Dammit?

Old joke:

The hardest part about
learning to ride a bike?

The Ground.

Once we realize the need to hit down it should become
simple, right? Well it seems there is a major deterrent to
hitting down. And it is called... the ground. In my years
of teaching this game, I have actually encountered very
little resistance to the theory of hitting down, once
explained. Now, what I have encountered has been a
lot of responses of" No one has ever told me that
before!" But once the theory has been explained, buying

into the theory has not been the problem. De-programming our fear of hitting the ground - for a hit down will mean such contact - has been the greater task.

In the act of hitting down at a golf ball that is sitting on the ground, it is virtually impossible not to hit the ground. However - especially when learning - we don't like the ground very much. It hasn't seemed right when we hit it, and when done incorrectly, it can feel really bad. So it is important to mention there is a right way and a wrong way to hit the ground. Ultimately these are related to when (at what point in the swing) we hit it, and from where (what angle).

"When" and "where" are in turn related to whether we are attempting to hit up, or hit down. Hitting the ground in an attempt to hit up can be very jarring. On the flipside, striking the ground after hitting down at the ball can produce a very smooth feeling. So smooth in fact, we often don't realize we hit the ground. This is a shame, because this misapprehension can dupe us into thinking we "picked" the ball clean, when in fact we didn't. A successful, yet unwitting, hit down, misperceived as a successful hit up, leads to what on the very next shot? Extra effort to hit up. And what does that lead to? Usually a very fat, or very thin shot.

Think about it. How many times in your golf life have you hit what seemed to be a perfect shot, and followed it up with a perfectly awful shot on the very next swing? Thought so.

So, how do we hit a golf ball with a downward swing, hitting the ground in such a way that it not only doesn't feel bad, but feels so good that you won't want to shut up about it at the dinner table? The picture becomes clearer once we have a basic understanding of both swing plane, and swing path.

Figure 6   Swing plane is determined by the angle of your club shaft at address.

As mentioned, many players associate hitting the ground with a negative feeling, physically. This negative feeling is a result of hitting the ground incorrectly; more specifically, at the wrong angle. If you pick your clubhead up vertically, and then drive it straight down into the ground it will imbed, much as an axe would when driven into apiece of wood. Such an action would be taking place on a vertical angle, or "plane".

"Swing plane" is essentially the "angle" on which the club (shaft) is being swung. In a golf swing there is an ideal plane on which to swing the golf club. This plane is determined by the angle of your club shaft at address. It is worth noting that the golf club manufacturers did not design golf clubs with the shaft coming out of the head vertically. Instead, the shaft comes out of the head at an angle (known as lie angle) such that the sole of the clubhead can sit flat on the ground while you stand holding the club to one side of the ball. A successful swing will see the club swung on

that same angle (plane) on the backswing, the downswing, and the follow-through. If the club is swung on the correct plane (a plane that is

Figure(s) 7   Your backswing and follow-through should be on the same plane.

consistent with the angle of the club shaft at address) the clubhead is able to hit the ground in such a way that it does not imbed, but rather it takes a divot and continues on its intended, natural path - known as "swing path". A club that is swung off its correct plane - particularly at an angle that is steeper than the intended plane - is very likely to imbed when contacting the ground, whether prior to, or post contact with the golf ball.

Conversely, if the club is swung on an overly " flat" plane, it is much less likely to hit the ground at all, and will produce a shot that is "thin" and/or goes significantly right of target.

20

3.2 Swing Path

It becomes easier to hit down when we know - better yet, can envision - correct swing path. Where swing plane is the angle the club shaft swings on, swing path is the exact route the head travels. For all intents and purposes it is a simple one. If you can imagine the traveling clubhead as an airplane leaving a trail of smoke, that smoke trail would draw the swing path of your golf club throughout the swing - back, down, and through.

The swing path starts with the clubhead in the address position, sitting on the target line. On the backswing

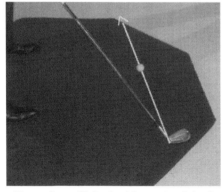

the clubhead travels NOT straight back along the target line, but rotates back, inside it. This will see the entire golf club (including shaft) parallel to the target line once the shaft is horizontal.

Figure 8   Club should not travel back along the target line.

As it is a rotation that gets it there, the clubhead will be in a position whereby the toe of the clubhead is pointing toward the sky. The face is NOT pointing down the target line, NOT pointing at the ground, but rather, parallel to the target line. As the club continues to swing (on plane) the swing path will see the clubhead travel up toward your right shoulder (NOT your right ear).

Subsequently, the downswing will see the clubhead travel down the path it came up.

Figure 9   *When club is horizontal, shaft is parallel to target line (not on it) and toe of clubhead is pointing skyward.*

The faster the clubhead travels down that path to the ball, the faster your clubhead speed will be at impact. As a result of the created momentum of the downswing, our physical position to one side of the target line, and the clubhead being attached to a shaft that has become attached to our arms, the path of the follow-through after impact will see the clubhead travel NOT straight up, NOT to the left, but away. Crossing the target line.

THIS IS IMPORTANT: The clubhead is not travelling down the target line. It is travelling from a point inside the target line, toward the target line. The natural laws of physics dictate that when an object is travelling - with speed - in a certain direction, it is not going to change directions unless forced or manipulated.

(We cannot force or manipulate a golf swing consistently. We are much better off to bow to the laws of physics which are consistent. This is where "let the clubhead do the work" is an invaluable rule to

Figure 10   The swing path will see the clubhead want to travel away...

remember.)

The problem we typically run into with this concept is essentially a "mental" one. We tend to struggle with the notion that a clubhead travelling from "inside" to "out", crossing the target line, can actually hit a straight shot down the target line. Yet this is exactly what happens in a good golf shot. Why?

Two reasons. The clubface will be square at impact, and... the fact the clubhead is rotating (pronating) promotes a right-to-left spin on the ball that will draw the ball back toward our ultimate target.

Figure 11 ...before it swings around to your left shoulder.

"But the club looks like it is swinging around to the left, doesn't it?" Yes. And it does. But not until it has exhausted its path to the right. When it has "run out of rope" so-to-speak. Then the clubhead has no choice but to swing around and over your left shoulder. Let's consider the shaft as a rope, and the clubhead as a tire attached to that rope. If you were to swing the tire from inside our target line, out towards the target line, would it magically turn left at the target line? No, it would cross the target line until the rope it is attached to is fully extended. It would then, and only then, swing around to the left.

Next to the concept of hitting down, this understanding of proper swing path is likely the most important lesson in the golf swing to grasp. As most golfers' chronic problem is hitting their shots to the right, most are just dying to steer the golf club around to the left at (or before) impact. Ironically, steering your club to the left is exactly what the "slice devil" would want you to do. The act of pulling or steering the club to the left aborts the rotation of the clubhead - the very rotation required to create a draw spin. Instead it causes the clubface to slide across the ball... in a right to left direction. What does that create? Left-to-right spin. And what is left-to-right spin? Slice spin. You got it.

Because of where you are swinging from (inside the target line) and to (the ball, which is on the target line) this action, this path, should occur naturally. You don't have to "remember" to swing out to the right. You do have to understand it, however. Buy into it -purely so you do not inadvertently sabotage your swing path. Allow physics to swing the club properly.

Gaining a clear understanding of where the club "wants" to go will stop you from steering to the left. As well, this full understanding will assist in your ability to hit down. It is very difficult to actively hit down if you have a hidden agenda of steering to the left, or trying to achieve a "high finish". Once you can envision a proper swing path, you can begin to actively promote speed in your downswing. Let Mother Nature take care of the rest. And yes, "Let the clubhead do the work!"

Hit Down Dammit!

3.3 The Follow-Through

In order to hit down correctly - taking a divot - it is necessary to swing the shaft of the club on plane and the clubhead on its proper path. Typically, when we do focus on swing plane it tends to be confined to the backswing and downswing. However, maintaining - or better yet, envisioning - correct plane on the follow-through is extremely important in furthering your ability to hit down.

Figure 12   An unforced follow-through will remain on plane.

A hit up at the ball will radically alter your swing plane on the follow-through, seeing the shaft rise vertically. .. rather than continuing on its original (correct) plane.

It is important to note that if the club is swung down correctly there will be no need to steer it through on its correct plane. The natural momentum of the clubhead and the angle on which it is being swung will see the club follow through on plane. If it is not following through on plane, we have a clear indication that the player is interfering with the natural path of the clubhead. In the overwhelming majority of cases this "interference" results from an attempt to physically strike up at the ball at impact, causing the golf club to deviate from its original plane.

26

Hitting down and allowing the golf club to follow through on plane allows the clubface to complete its rotation through the golf ball. This creates the requisite right-to-left spin necessary to prevent a shot that ultimately goes to the right (due to predominant left to right spin). It is important (necessary) to swing the golf club "on plane" in order to hit good shots.

When we speak of hitting down we speak of hitting down the plane, *not* vertically down at the golf ball. Vertically hitting down at the ball will lead to the imbedding effect that instills a fear of hitting the ground. In order to avoid this, it is important to understand what faults may cause us to hit down vertically...

Chapter 4

The Evils of Hitting Down Vertically

A vertical "attack" (what we do not want) at the golf ball is generally caused in two ways. One is influenced by the route and size of our backswing, the other in the manner we start our downswing...

4.1 The Backswing

A good "on plane" backswing is a result of:

Figure 13   This "big backswing" loses distance, rather than gaining it.

a) Understanding the club needs to swing on plane and what that plane is, and…

b) Arms and body working together.

By putting too much emphasis on a big backswing, many players find themselves negatively altering their backswing plane after their body has finished turning. This happens when they continue their backswing further, using their arms exclusively to raise the club even higher. This produces a steep swing plane that, barring any magical rerouting of the club on the way down, will produce a very steep angle of attack at the golf ball. Whether intending to "hit down" or not, this angle of attack is most likely going to see the golf club:

Imbed in the ground,

or…

Having discovered the unpleasantness of such an effect, pull up before the clubhead reaches the ball, and either miss the ball, top it, or hit it thin.

29   *Hit Down Dammit!*

There are three components to a good back swing. Getting the club to horizontal is not one of them.

Getting the club to horizontal may (or may not) be a result of having achieved all three components. The components are:

1) Weight on the right (back) foot;

2) Back to the target;

3) Clubhead higher than hands.

Achieving one of the aforementioned, even perfectly, without having achieved the other two components, will lead to a seriously flawed backswing. Typically, there is such a great emphasis on a huge backswing that none of the three components is achieved because:

i)   In the huge backswing rotation, weight shifts from the front foot to the back foot, and to the front foot again (reverse pivot). A downswing that starts with your weight on the front foot will see your weight now shift the wrong way, to the back foot, when everything else is moving forward! This will cost you power, not create it.

ii)   The over-rotation of the backswing will see your

back not facing the target, but rather to the right of target. Guess where the ball is going to go?

iii)   And finally, the huge backswing will typically see your club go past horizontal, where the clubhead is now below your hands. It is virtually impossible to successfully hit up or down from this position. Your hands will have so much work to do in order to have the clubhead catch up to the rest of your body, that even if achieved the result will be a hands only swipe at the ball. Not powerful at all.

A further note of importance about the backswing re: tempo. The function of the backswing is simply to set up ("load") the downswing. That's it. I like to equate the backswing to backing out of your driveway. If you are late for work (or the golf course) quickly backing out of your driveway will not get you to your destination much quicker. But it may very well get you into an accident. You want to back your car out smoothly, change gears (to forward) and then... zoom...accelerate! Same with your backswing. A slow smooth backswing, then change gears to... hit down.

Now to the downswing...

4.2 The Downswing

The other contributor to a steep angle of attack (hitting down vertically) is the fruitless attempt to create power by "pulling" the handle of the golf club to initiate the downswing. This error begins at the top of the backswing. Once reaching the top, in an effort to "hit"

as hard as possible we mistakenly pull the handle of the club downwards quickly. We seem to understand that "quick" will create power, but forget that it is the clubhead that needs to move quickly.

As soon as the handle is pulled down, the plane of your downswing

Figure 14   Pulling on the handle throws the clubhead 'over the top'.

will change radically, forcing the head to a very steep position from which to attack.

While seemingly obvious, it is worth planting in our minds that we are hitting the ball with the clubhead, and it is the clubhead that needs to move quickly. Pulling hard on the handle will not only cause the swing to come off plane and attack from a steep angle, but will retard the speed of the clubhead as it remains "trapped" behind the handle. In order to enhance clubhead speed we need to swing the clubhead down, NOT PULL the handle down. The head needs to be pushed down the path it came up. This will be done not

by pulling the handle, but using the handle to essentially lever the clubhead down its natural path. The club needs to move fast from the outside (head), not the inside (handle) in order to hit the ball a considerable distance. This will then also facilitate the return of

Figure 15   Club has not been 'released'. Shaft is not extended toward target, clubface still wide open.

the clubface to its square address position at impact. In a correct swing, the clubhead will be moving so fast that after impact it will speed well by the handle and into a position whereby the shaft is now extended toward the target (parallel to the target line) and the clubhead will have rotated to what is commonly known as a "toe-up" position. When the handle is pulled down in a vain attempt to create power, the clubhead will actually lag behind the handle, trapped; never accumulating enough speed to pass the handle or rotate back to square. Post impact, we will see the club has not achieved the desired "released" position, the shaft will be perpendicular to the target line (as opposed to parallel) and the face relatively wide open.

Hit Down Dammit!

The downswing is everything in the golf swing. The backswing positions us to make a downswing. The follow through is a result of the downswing. The downswing is the 'nuts and bolts'. If any effort is to be expended in your swing, the downswing is where it should occur. This is your opportunity to "invest" in clubhead speed. A little effort invested at the beginning of the downswing can pay off significantly in terms of clubhead speed at the ball. All too often we wait until the clubhead gets to the ball and then we apply effort - upward. Too little, too late, wrong direction.

While I liken the backswing to backing out of your driveway, I analogize the downswing in terms of a retirement investment. The top of your backswing is your 18th birthday. The golf ball: your 65th birthday. The downswing represents your effective working years. A small financial investment on your 18th birthday can translate into huge dividends by retirement. In the golf swing, waiting until your clubhead reaches the ball and then applying effort upwards is like waiting until your 64th birthday to invest in your retirement. It would take a lot, and the payoff would be minimal.

Chapter 5

The Art of Hitting Down

Hit Down Dammit!

5.1 The Thrust

Figure 16   Half-backswing position. The nucleus of the golf swing is from waist-high on the backswing, to waist-high on the follow-through.

The art of hitting down is best learned from a half backswing position. The ideal position will see the clubshaft approximately waist-high and parallel to the target line. The toe of the clubhead should be pointing skyward. In this position, your left arm will be reasonably extended but more importantly, your right arm and right wrist will be bent.

DO NOT confuse bending and straightening the right wrist with having a "wristy" swing. The rationale is this: your address position is your desired impact position. At address your right wrist was straight. On your backswing you will bend your right wrist back (commonly known as "cocking" or "setting" your wrist). In order to return to your address position at impact you MUST straighten that right wrist!

A typical, erroneous, first move is to "pull" the butt of

the club toward the target to start the downswing. This is what we will endeavour to "un-train". Through effort and repetition, we will learn rather to thrust the clubhead down toward the golf ball. This will be done essentially with the simultaneous straightening of the right arm and wrist. Yes, even the wrist. This straightening of the right wrist and arm (key factors in achieving extension) is necessary to return the clubface to square, and has the added benefit of creating extra, uncontested

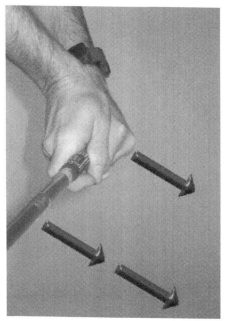

Figure 17   Straightening the cocked right wrist delivers (thrusts) the clubhead to the ball. The longer the shaft, the faster the clubhead will go.

clubhead speed to your downswing.

This is no different than throwing a ball. First, try throwing a ball without bending your right arm and wrist on the "backswing". Not easy, is it? Now, bend your right wrist and arm on the backswing as you normally would for a throw. Throw the ball without straightening your right arm or right wrist. Feel kinda geeky? Don't be doing this in public if you want to preserve your reputation!

Hit Down Dammit!

This thrusting action of the right hand and arm in a throw is the same for the downswing of a golf shot. If you fail to straighten your right wrist or arm on the downswing you will fail to return the clubface to square, fail to accumulate clubhead speed, fail to hit good golf shots. And remember, this action does not stop at the ball. When thrusting, "plow through" the ball. Often we make effort to the ball, but not through it. If our hitting action stops at the ball, this must have been preceded by some form of deceleration prior to reaching the ball. If a club is decelerating when it should be doing the opposite - accelerating - it is easy to see the effect this will have on clubhead speed (and therefore distance). The act of "braking" at the ball also nullifies rotation of the clubhead, thus reduction (or elimination) of the right to left spin required to avoid a slice, and gain a draw.

5.2 The Path of the Hit Down

A vital key to achieving the aforementioned thrusting motion is that the clubhead must be thrust down the intended swing path. If you deviate from this path (such as to get under and hit up, or by steering to the left in the hopes of avoiding a shot to the right) your shot will NOT be successful.

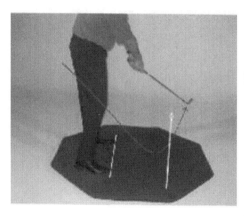

Figure 18 The clubhead travelled from the first white line - near the body - to the second (target line) which is away from the body. Its momentum will see it continue away until it has reached 'the end of its rope'.

Let's talk a little about this portion of the swing path. For all intents and purposes it is a straight line down to the ball. This straight line starts from reasonably well inside the target line, and works out toward the target line. It does NOT work up and down the target line, as much as we might think it ought to. As mentioned, one of the common causes of a deviation from proper swing path is an attempt to steer the clubhead around to the left. We do this because we sense we are coming from inside the target line, and imagine that we need to somehow sling the club back to the left in order to stop the golf ball from shooting to the right. Wrong. We actually want to encourage the club's natural momentum out to the ball (and beyond).

Hit Down Dammit!

Any attempt to "steer" to the left will negate this.

Consider the angle of approach of the clubhead to the ball. It is not "down the line" but from inside it, and out to the line. Now consider the momentum of the speeding clubhead. Were the clubhead allowed to continue along its line of approach we would see that line continue out beyond the target line, to the right. In other words, if the clubhead were to come unglued and fly off the shaft at impact its line of momentum would see it fly to the right. The reason the ball will not fly directly to the right is because the clubface will be square at impact. The motion from inside the line to out may create a certain right-to-left spin on the golf ball, commonly known as a "draw". This will see the ball start a little right of its target, and then move (spin) back toward it.

5.3 Steering Into Trouble

Ironically, any attempt to arbitr~
clubhead back to the left will cause the ~
(slice) to the right, with an accompanying loss
power. This slicing action will take place even with a
square clubface, although usually the attempt to steer
prevents rotation of the clubface to square and
exacerbates the problem, exaggerating the ball flight to
the right of target.

*Figure 19   Extending across the target line
promotes 'draw'(right-to-left) spin.*

Alternatively - but again when attempting to steer the clubhead around to the left - the hands may "snap" the face of the club shut (closed) prior to, or at, impact. This causes a drastic "snap hook" to the left.

A variance in the result of trying to steer may even lead to a series of shots that go left one minute, right the next, but never straight. This is one of the most annoying symptoms of bad golf because there is no way to predict, or even compensate for, the direction of your ensuing shot. As you can imagine, it becomes very difficult to line up when you have no idea if your mistake will go dead right or drastically left! Generally

Hit Down Dammit!

teering action "kicks in" at impact. Unwittingly, u don't swing down as hard as you could because you are saving "effort" for the last second steer to the left.

One answer to "steering" lies in promoting speed in your downswing. An accelerating downswing should create enough momentum in the descending clubhead that it flies down and through the ball, crossing the target line, only coming around to the left (your left shoulder) when its path to the right has been exhausted - after full extension has been achieved.

5.4 The Deathly Dip

No, we are not talking about rancid liverwurst. Another common deviation from the natural downward swing path is caused by a premature "dip" - or dropping of the clubhead -behind the ball in an unwitting readiness to strike up at it. This is often caused because we imagine we need to create a curve in the downswing, in order to "scoop" the ball up.

Figure 20 Picture the path to the ball as a straight line, and you will stop hitting behind the ball.

No doubt, the path of the clubhead to the ball will be a curving one. But for all intents and purposes **we must see the line to the golf ball as being straight**. We must attempt to accelerate the clubhead to the ball in the straightest line possible in order not to deviate from the natural path to the ball.

While we acknowledge it is a curved path, any attempt to arbitrarily create a curve will do nothing but exaggerate that curve. This will see the bottom of the arc suddenly move to appoint well behind the ball, leaving you no option but to strike up, or laterally, at it. If you picture the line to the ball as a straight one, in

Hit Down Dammit!

your effort to strike down that line you will naturally take the clubhead on a curving path -due to the nature of our set-up, the angle of the shaft from the clubhead, and the fact it is being swung from a "pivot" - or axle; specifically: *you.*

Figure 21   Club has 'dipped' (dropped behind ball) leaving no opportunity to hit down. Note: weight has shifted backward rather than forward.

5.5 The Role of the Hands

Apart from our brain, our hands are perhaps the most unique and advanced characteristic of the human species. Our hands play a very important role in swinging a golf club, and especially in hitting down. Particularly the right hand.

In our drill position where the club is approximately waist high (parallel to the target line, and toe up)your right hand should be more or less on top of the club. What it must NOT be is "under" the club (as it might be if you have what is ironically known as a "strong" grip).

Figure(s) 22 Looking down at half backswing position: Left wrist has rotated, right wrist has cocked, ready to uncock/thrust downward.

For the sake of this exercise, from this position your first move will be to use the right hand to push the bottom half of the golf club (i.e. the clubhead) down to the golf ball. At first this will not be easy, as you may well find your instinct is to pull the handle of the club to the left, or toward the ultimate target. The purpose of this exercise is to un-train this incorrect habit. Because we (wrongly) associate "pulling" with power in the golf swing our tendency is to pull the club toward the target. However, such an action: does not create speed with the clubhead; does not allow the clubface to rotate back to square; creates a lateral approach to the ball which will negate the angle of attack a downward strike creates, leading to a low ball flight; often causes the hosel(or "shank") of the club to reach the ball before the clubface causing... that's right, a shank; leads to the clubface being pulled from right to left across the ball, creating a cut or a slice.

5.51 Right Hand Thrust Drill

Repeatedly swing your club back to waist-high, pause a split second, then use your right hand to "thrust" the clubhead toward the ball. In doing so, you may find you have created sufficient speed with the clubhead that it follows through to the target automatically, leaving you in a finish position whereby the clubhead is pointing at the target, the toe is up, and the shaft is roughly horizontal (waist-high) and parallel to the target line. This position should roughly mirror your top of-backswing position.

As you get more proficient at this exercise, you will create more clubhead speed, the momentum from which will see a follow-through that "naturally" swings through a little higher than the height of your backswing. It is important this follow through is natural - neither forced nor abbreviated.

Learn to swing from this position...

hit down...

and follow through to this position.

5.6 Adding Motion to Motion

So why does this slight acceleration of the clubhead with the hands contribute so significantly to distance? And with seemingly so little effort? Again, it is worth re-stating that clubhead speed = distance.

By using your hands effectively in the golf swing you are essentially gaining the benefit of adding motion... to motion. We can put this into perspective by thinking of an escalator, and an adjacent set of stairs at your local department store.

Consider a person walking normally up the stairs, and imagine the speed they would likely be moving. Then consider someone standing on the escalator, and imagine their speed. Now, imagine someone walking normally up the moving escalator, and how quickly they appear to be - in fact are - moving. The escalator is not moving any faster, nor is the individual walking any faster. But the combination of the individual's motion and the motion of the escalator - motion on motion - nets out to a significant increase in speed. The person simply walking up the stairs would have to walk much faster - requiring more effort - in order to keep up. Or, the escalator would have to run at a faster speed - requiring more energy - in order for the person who is standing on it to match the greater speed of the combined "motion on motion".

We all know that the arms and body create motion in the golf swing. The trouble is in order to create faster motion we tend to swing the body and arms harder, and leave the hands docile. This would not be effective in throwing a ball, and it is no more effective in a golf swing.

5.61 Throwing the Ball Drill

You will not require a golf club for this drill. Rather, you will need a golf ball in your right hand, and a mark placed on the ground slightly forward of your typical ball position, and outside the target line. Now set up as if to hit a golf ball. Make a backswing wherein your right hand and arm will rotate back to your right shoulder.

Figure(s) 23   This is a throwing action, not a 'skipping-stone' action.

Now throw the ball at the mark you have placed on the ground. This action will essentially replicate the role of your

right side in a golf shot, and give you the distinct sensation associated with hitting down. Notice that in trying to hit the mark there is no "upward" effort in any way.

Notice too the extension of your right arm and wrist. Notice the thrusting action to a point that is slightly right of the target line. Once you have become comfortable with the drill and are more or less hitting your target consistently, try throwing the ball a little harder. It won't be difficult to do. To really highlight the point, you may even want to swing your right hand (holding the golf ball) up to your right shoulder, then swing down but try to throw the ball "up" into the air. Watch you don't hit yourself in the head. You will note your success will be less, while your embarrassment will be great.

Figure 24   Right arm thrusting down, weight has shifted to front foot, 100 mph slapshot.

One summer afternoon, a father and son were at my practice range. The father stopped hitting for a moment to instruct his son, commenting that the golf swing "isn't a hockey slapshot." Unfortunately the father was not able to see the forest for the trees: his son was hitting the ball better than he was.

The action of a golf shot does share a key ingredient with the hockey slapshot. In both actions, the key is to hit down. Both the slap and golf shot actions share the physical requirement of hitting down in order to raise their respective puck or ball. What is interesting to note is the psychological difference. As stated in chapter one, in golf we are somewhat duped into hitting up by the fact the ball is round, and the clubface is angled back. In hockey, on the other hand, the puck is perfectly flat, as is the ice surface. The blade of the hockey stick is angled slightly forward rather than back. What this does in hockey is takeaway the notion that we are supposed - or even able - to get under the puck to raise it. With no foreseeable way of getting under the puck, a hockey player takes the next most logical approach and that is to hit down at it.

While the psychology in golf is different, the reality is not. In order to hit a successful, powerful shot in golf, we need to hit down.

5.71 Split-Grip Drill

The "split-grip" is possibly the greatest drill in golf that does not come in a box, you don't have to buy the video, there's no monthly installments, you don't pay extra for a famous instructor's endorsement, and no batteries are required. In fact, you do not even need golf balls as this is purely a practice swing" feel" drill.

Figure 25   There should be a distinct "gap" between your hands.

The split-grip: simply grip the club with your left hand as per normal, but place your right hand at the bottom of the grip. This will leave a distinct space between your two hands. Lower the club to the ground and, maintaining the split-grip, begin to make practice swings. Swing the club up, and note how automatically your right side wants to hit down. As you do hit down - contacting the ground solidly each time - you will see how the clubhead wants to fly through to the target, and may even pull you off-balance at first attempt.

If you do feel off-balance this does not mean you are doing the drill incorrectly, but rather that you are now transferring your weight forward in away you are not accustomed to.

Conditions you should be aware of in this drill include

a distinct folding of the right arm as you swing the club up. If in your normal golf swing you attempt to take the club back too low and down the target line, you will feel this is now awkward to do with the split-grip drill. If you are accustomed to keeping your right arm bent on the downswing (a nasty by-product of trying to keep your right elbow "tucked") you will likely fail to hit the ground, and maintaining balance will become unachievable, even with repetition.

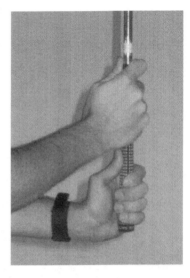

Figure 26 Back of left hand and palm of right hand facing target, as in any good grip.

One day I was teaching some very young juniors. I had them hitting off driving range mats, and they were not allowed to use a tee as I did not want them to getaway with hitting up.

However, one of the kids was placing the ball in the hole of the mat (where a rubber tee would normally be). I began to tell him not to do that, as it would make the shot too difficult - until I noticed he was hitting the ball surprisingly well. By somewhat submerging the ball he had taken away any notion of getting under the ball to hit it. Instead, he was intuitively striking DOWN at the ball to" pop" it up. Despite the poor lie he had created for himself, he was hitting very good shots.

Five minutes later I had the entire group hitting golf balls out of the hole in their respective range mats, and they were hitting down wonderfully - preventing me from having to say *"Hit Down Dammit!"* to such young tender ears.

Chapter 6

Facts vs. Clichés

Even if your exposure to this game has been limited so far, it is a safe bet you have already been introduced to some of our more "well-worn" clichés. And if you are a veteran of the game, let's see if you aren't guilty of using some of these clichés.

Generally these clichés are band-aid attempts to correct symptoms associated with poor ball striking. You can chase after symptoms until the cows come home but unless you start addressing the cause of a bad swing you can never develop a good one. The symptom correcting approach to golf is tantamount to your doctor discovering you have a bad cold, and then telling you to stop coughing. Unless you treat the cause of the cold, the best result you can hope for is an extended stay in bed watching The Golf Channel.

Here are some of the more common clichés, and a look at the likely "cause" of the symptom they are trying to fix...

6.1 You Lifted Your Head?

How many times have you been told (or perhaps even told someone else) that the cause of your errant shot was lifting your head? We hear it all the time, and it is probably the single most common symptom of a poor shot. But the truth is...

**Almost never is a bad shot
the result of lifting your head.**

Figure 27 Nothing will keep your head down as effectively as hitting down.

The bad shot was in fact the result of your body driving up at the golf ball. If your head is attached to your body, the force of driving up will cause your head to come up too. This creates the perception that you lifted your head.

In an effort to hit up at the ball you lifted your body. You will discover that as you learn to hit down, it is very difficult to lift your head as all your physical action will be working down through the ball.

6.2 Keep Your Eye On The Ball?

Keep your eye on the ball. Good advice. And easy to do
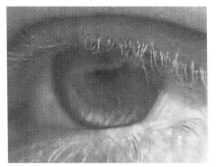
if you are hitting down. But if instinctively you are swinging UP at the ball, you will find it very difficult to keep your eye on it no matter how hard you try.

Think about it. The ball is below you. You begin by looking at it. You must swing back and... hit down at the object you are looking at. In doing this, keeping your eye on the ball suddenly becomes much easier to achieve. Try looking down at something you are trying to hit up at! That is far more difficult - and if that is what you are doing, it becomes obvious why it may seem so difficult to keep your eye on the ball. It becomes easy to keep your eye on the ball... when you hit down.

Hit Down Dammit!

6.3 Sweep The Ball?

This is a well-intentioned - yet very dangerous - piece of advice. Why? Well, what do you do after you make a mess? Sweep up? Or sweep down? The notion of sweeping the ball is only going to encourage you to hit UP, and will bring with it all the negative side-effects of such an action.

This advice is supposed to discourage you from chopping at the ball, or have the clubhead rise too quickly after impact (a result of hitting up).

Figure 28   Sweeping the ball will tend to send the ball low, making it difficult to get in the air.

What a sweeping action can cause is a very low take-away, and a resulting low approach to the ball making it extremely difficult to hit down. This almost lateral path of the clubhead will result in a low ball flight, if not a skull. This questionable advice is typically dispensed when we are hitting long irons or fairway woods - which already go low - that we seem to hit up at even more desperately in order to create height on the shot. Sweeping is not the answer. Hitting down is.

6.4 Finish High?

Sadly, the encouragement of a "high finish" is one of the most misleading directions in golf. Telling someone to strive for a high finish with their golf swing is tantamount to giving them a license to hit up.

Figure 29 A "high finish" takes the club off plane and off its natural path, affecting both distance and direction.

The common interpretation of a high finish is not one that is consistent with staying on plane. And certainly it will cause the clubhead to deviate from its natural path. A player that tries to finish high will, at impact, suddenly thrust the clubhead upwards vertically and therefore off its original swing plane. In preparation for this sudden change in swing path the clubhead is not allowed to accelerate downwards fully, nor rotate back to square. The result will generally include:

- the ball going right;
  - lack of distance;
    - a skull shot;
    - or a fat hit.

The well-meaning intention behind encouraging a high finish is two-fold:

a) to dissuade players who typically hit the ball to the right from trying to steer it to the left (and thus what would appear to be a low finish) and:

b) to counter a player's failure to follow-through.

In each of these cases there is a reason the ball is going to the right (pulling the handle for power, or no follow-through as clubhead is trapped behind the handle being pulled) and that is what must be remedied, as opposed to a symptomatic solution such as "finish high".

6.5 Don't Move Your Head?

One of the most revered instructions in golf, and yet perhaps the most ridiculous. Write down in the box below all the sports that you can play without moving your head:

```
┌─────────┐
│         │
└─────────┘
```

Done?

Golf is an athletic endeavour. It requires a symphony of moving parts. If your head is even loosely attached to any of these parts it too must move. So why do we insist that the head not move? Simply because when we hit up our head comes up too. Guilt by association. The intent behind not moving your head is simply that if it does not move, it becomes more difficult to hit up and therefore hit a bad shot. However, consciously hitting down eradicates the need for such a dangerous direction.

One of the worst side-effects associated with an attempt (or even success) to keep one's head still is the dreaded "reverse pivot" (fig. 13, pg. 29). This is where your weight shifts from the middle (at address) and around to the front foot, rather than to the back foot where it should be, on the backswing. This happens because refusing to move your head prevents your weight from moving to the right, so instead your weight effectively rotates around with your hips and shoulders... to...your front foot.

Hit Down Dammit!

To add insult to injury, as you swing the club forward your weight now shifts to the back foot in preparation for a hefty old swipe up at the golf ball, but at a time when it should be shifting forward for power, not back for hitting up!

6.6 Your Right Hand Goes Along For The Ride?

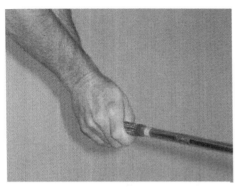

Figure 30   The properly positioned right hand is instrumental in hitting down.

In the contest for the most baffling piece of swing advice, this one must rank at or near the top. I have often found a student to struggle not with the concept of hitting down, but rather, the execution - only to find that they had a "hidden agenda" of keeping their right hand (often their entire right side) passive throughout the golf swing. They were relying almost entirely on their left arm(and side) to swing the golf club. Whenever I encounter this I ask why it is one would even consider entering into an athletic endeavour using their weaker, less-coordinated arm? Usually the answer amounts to, "Um, because I read somewhere that the right hand just goes for the ride." Hello?

The vast majority of golfers are right handed. Even in Canada. And the vast majority of these golfers play golf right-handed. This is for a reason. We need our stronger, more coordinated side to swing a golf club down and through a golf ball. If you doubt this, perform the following test. You will need twenty golf balls. Using your right arm only, swing and hit ten of the balls, one at a time. Now hit the remaining ten using your left arm only. With which arm were you consistently more successful, and which way "felt" easier?

(No time like the present to apologize to all the lefties out there. You are no doubt accustomed to much of the golf industry favouring right-handers and I regret this book has done the same, for obvious reasons. If you are indeed a natural left-handed playing golfer (i.e. you are left handed and play golf left handed) then you can simply switch right for left throughout this instruction. If you are naturally left-handed but play golf right handed – a common case for those who grew up when there was very limited left handed golf equipment choices – you may find you need to work harder on developing the right side in your golf swing. Or, and I am not kidding, consider switching back to playing golf left-handed, with your naturally stronger and more coordinated side playing its proper role in the golf swing. CS)

6.61 Right Arm Only Drill

Practicing regularly with a right-arm-only drill is useful in more ways than one. If you are prone to the "chicken wing" follow-through, you will note it is the left arm that is the culprit. Essentially the use of the left arm to "pull" the club through prevents it from rotating, and thus from getting out of the way to allow a proper follow through. Swinging with your right arm only literally eradicates this problem, and allows you to feel

what it is like to swing the clubhead through on its proper path. The fact you are swinging with one arm as opposed to two may change the way you strike the ball from a "hit" to a "swing". With two arms we feel like Goliath, and tend to muscle the ball.

Figure 31   With one arm, the notion of" hitting up" seems less feasible so instead we encourage the clubhead to accelerate "down" toward the ball allowing – as the cliché goes - the club to do the work.

With one arm we are David, and resort to strategy - such as using the weight of the club, gravity, and centripetal force to "swing" the club as opposed to "hit" with it. Remember, it is relatively easy - even with one arm - to push a clubhead down when it is naturally heading downward already. It is something else altogether to arbitrarily redirect a descending object upward, and attempting to do so with one-arm-only illustrates this point convincingly.

6.7 Hit Up With Your Driver?

No.

Better yet, why?

Gravity is not suddenly going to work upwards just because you have a driver in your hand. You are not suddenly going to be able to redirect a bigger, descending clubhead upwards at the exact bottom of the arc and keep the clubhead on its swing path and the club on plane.

The whole reason we hit a driver, let's face it, is purely for distance. And what produces distance? That's right, clubhead speed. And when is the clubhead going the fastest? On the downswing.

Why do so many people slice their driver, even if they do not slice their other clubs? The act of hitting up with the driver (or any club, for that matter) prevents the natural pronation of the clubhead, the pronation that promotes right to left spin – draw spin. Hitting up, the clubhead does not pronate, rather it slides across the ball from right to left (creating left to right spin – slice spin). The more you hit up, the more you slice.

Do not let the fact the ball is on a tee fool you. It is not an invitation to hit up at the ball. The swing is the swing is the swing. Develop one good, repeating, swing and you can hit any club in your bag.

Pre-impact:

Impact:

Post-impact:

Hitting down led to a green jacket!

71 *Hit Down Dammit!*

Chapter 7

Common Complaints

Take a pen and a piece of paper, and jot down the most prevalent problems you experience with your golf shots. Now compare them to the list below, containing the most common complaints I hear as a teacher.

1. All my bad shots go to the right;

2. I can't get the ball up in the air (all my shots go low or I top them);

3. I don't get enough distance;

4. All my clubs go the same distance;

5. I keep hitting the ground before the ball;

6. My shots are inconsistent;

7. I hit my short irons fine, it's my long irons and woods I have difficulty with;

8. I can hit my irons off the fairway, but not my fairway woods.

How many of the symptoms from this list pertain to you? Let's look at each one briefly, and discuss their relationship to hitting up rather than hitting down.

The act of hitting up at a golf ball requires an action that causes the clubhead to deviate from its natural swing path. A proper swing path will see the leading edge of the clubface square with the target line at address. It will ROTATE open to a position parallel to the target line on the backswing (when the shaft is parallel to the target line and level with the horizon, toe pointing skyward), ROTATE BACK to square at impact, and then continue to rotate to a position parallel to the target line again on the follow through (shaft parallel to the target line and the horizon, toe pointing skyward).

Figure 32 Clubhead is rising too quickly, face is still open, shaft has not been released, right wrist still bent. By staying "on the target line" club has moved away from power source, clubhead has not rotated. Shaft should be parallel to target line, not touching it.

The swing path of a hitting up action will not see the clubhead return to square at impact. Rather it will remain open as the clubhead rises straight up, causing the ball to fly to the right. The perception of the relative "squareness" of the clubface on the follow through can be very deceiving here, because an upswing will leave the clubface in a position that appears to be square with the target line.

However, after impact we do not want the clubface to be square with the target line, we want it to be square with you, and you should now be facing your target (whereas at address you were side on to it). The same applies to your backswing. Despite the perceived logic of keeping the clubface on, and square to, the target line on your backswing, doing so is actually:

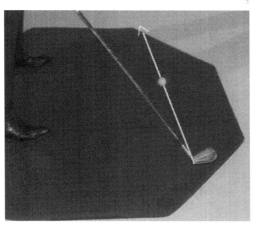

a) moving the clubhead away from its power source (you),

b) keeping the face shut, and

c) preventing rotation of the clubhead as it is swung back.

Figure 33 By staying 'on the target line' club has moved away from power source, clubhead has not rotated. Shaft should be parallel to target line, not touching it.

We have to accept that, unlike bowling, our body is not pointing down the target line. Rather, we are side-on to our intended target. For so long as we stand to one side of the golf ball (and therefore the target line) we must accept that the clubhead will swing back INSIDE the target line on the way up, swing out and beyond the target line on the way down, and finally swing back inside the target line after impact. In fact, the clubface will be square with the target line for a relatively brief period of time - but when it counts ... at impact.

Consider a swinging door you might see at the entrance to a kitchen in a restaurant. Let's say the handle of the door is your clubface, pointing at your intended target (and therefore on our imaginary target line). At rest, the door is square. When it opens, the outer edge of the door (and the handle) does NOT go straight back down the target line, but rather it rotates inside. Then upon closing it rotates again, this time in the reverse direction but on exactly the same path as when it opened. And where is the door when it reaches the closed position? Square again. Each and every time.

7.2 I Can't Get the Ball Up In The Air

This section could also be called: *"All My Shots Go Low or I Top Them"*. Low and topped golf shots are a result of the clubhead rising - rather than descending - at impact. Generally, the rising leading edge (or lowest portion of the clubface) makes contact with the equator or upper half of the golf ball causing the ball to spin

forward and low, rather than back and up. Consider the execution of a topspin shot in tennis - the racket attacks the ball from below, with a sharp upward strike that then spins the ball forward rather than backward. A very

Figure 34 Clubhead rising at impact creates what is known as a 'topped' shot.

useful shot in tennis - sadly, not so useful in golf.

In extreme circumstances the leading edge will catch the equator dead on, resulting in what is known as a "skulled" shot that shoots out extremely low and along the ground. This is often accompanied by a stinging or numbing of the hands as this kind of contact forces your hands to absorb the vibrations of the impact. In the most extreme of circumstances - the topped shot - the sole of the rising clubhead will hit the absolute top of the golf ball on the way up, essentially pounding the ball downwards and a minimal distance.

Often, a "topped shot" is misperceived as the bottom (or

the leading edge) of the club hitting the top of the ball on the way *down*. This of course dupes us into associating "hitting down" with a negative result. You may want to go to the length of watching a close up video of your clubhead when you top a shot... seeing the clubhead rise just prior to impact in order to sell the message to our always dubious subconscious. In a correct downward hit the club will contact the ground just after impact, allowing the ground - rather than you -to absorb the vibrations of impact.

Figure 35 The clubhead is moving its fastest on the way down.

If I haven't said it yet, I'll say it now: clubhead speed =distance. The faster your clubhead is moving at impact, the further the ball will travel. Your clubhead is moving its fastest as it is descending, peaking at the bottom of the swing arc. Your clubhead is beginning to slowdown as it rises from the bottom of the arc. To hit the golf ball on the way up is to hit the golf ball as the clubhead is slowing down. That alone will cost you distance.

The act of intentionally re-directing the clubhead at impact in order to hit up at the ball means that the accelerating forces of gravity and centrifugal force are negated, causing a deceleration in clubhead speed. Any contact with the ground prior to contact with the golf ball will obviously reduce effective clubhead speed at impact, and therefore distance. Hitting up costs you distance. Conversely, *increased* clubhead speed will add distance to your shots. When is the best opportunity to accelerate the clubhead? On the way down. Even a slight acceleration of the clubhead at the TOP or your downswing will multiply out to significantly increased speed at the bottom.

Consider a retirement investment. Are you better off to make a small contribution to your retirement at the age of 18, and then see that investment multiply until the pay off at 65? Or is it better to wait until you are 64 and be forced to make a big investment, that even then only has one year to grow? Waiting to reach the bottom of your swing arc to apply power in an upward direction is tantamount to investing at 64. A slight acceleration of the clubhead as it begins its descent (not hard to do as it is going down anyway)is like investing at 18, and the payoff is huge.

Figure 36   Wouldn't it be so much easier if they needed to push the car down the hill?

Another analogy...Would you rather push a car down a hill, or up one? And if you were to push it down a hill (with the goal of achieving ultimate speed) would you give it an extra push at the top of the hill, or wait until it reached the bottom to give it that extra nudge? (If the latter, be sure your health/life insurance is all paid up.)

7.4 All My Clubs Go the Same Distance

Two attributes of a golf club affect the distance a ball

will travel. One is the length of the club. The longer the club, the faster the head will travel when swung properly. The other attribute is the loft of the club. The more loft a club has, the higher the trajectory of the well-hit shot. The higher trajectory leads to a more vertical

Figure 37 The loft of the club affects trajectory primarily when hitting down at the ball.

drop of the golf ball once it has reached its peak altitude, and therefore less roll upon landing. The lower the trajectory, the greater the roll and therefore added distance.

By design, the shorter clubs (7, 8, 9) have more loft (combining slower clubhead speed with a higher trajectory shot) whereas longer clubs (3, 4, 5) have less loft (combining greater clubhead speed with lower trajectory and more roll, for even more distance).

However, the true, effective loft of the golf club only comes into play when the clubhead strikes the ball in a downward manner. As described earlier, when the club strikes down the ball becomes trapped momentarily between the clubface and the ground. Having nowhere else to go the ball spins backwards up the lofted clubface at an angle dictated by the degree of loft. More loft, higher launch angle; less loft, lower launch. But if the club is striking up at the time of impact, essentially we have a flat piece of metal thrusting upward at the golf ball. The effect of the loft of the clubface is diminished, and the height of the shot is now more influenced by the angle at which we are thrusting. Regardless of the club we are using, the resultant shots will be similar.

Even the effect of progressive clubhead speed from short to long irons is minimized as general clubhead speed is less when hitting up, and significantly reduced if the clubhead contacts the ground prior to impact. When consistently hitting down at the golf ball, the incremental differences in loft and shaft length are maximized from club to club, resulting in desired incremental differences in distance and trajectory as well.

7.51 Keep Hitting The Ground Before The Ball

Hitting the ground before the ball is commonly known as hitting "fat". Hitting the ball "fat" is generally attributed to a failure to shift your weight from the back foot to the front foot. While failing to shift your weight will cause you to hit the ball fat, the problem will not be solved until we acknowledge WHY you are not shifting your weight.

Just telling you to shift your weight is generally not enough. Why? Because hitting the ground before the ball is one of the most devastating results - and significant indicators - of an attempt to hit up at the golf ball. If you are of a mindset to hit up in order to get the ball airborne, an instruction telling you to shift your weight will usually result in your striking up at the golf ball - with your weight on the wrong foot - followed by an ineffective weight shift after the ball has departed (probably not very far, probably to the right, but gone nonetheless).

Figure 38   If you are consistently hitting behind the ball, chances are you are trying to hit up.

Unfortunately, in so many cases the failure to shift your weight, or your failure to hit

Hit Down Dammit!

the ball without hitting the ground first, is wrongly interpreted as resulting from lack of talent, athletic ability, or hand-eye coordination. Yet it is intriguing how many students who previously suffered from "ground-before-ballitus" (who literally missed the ball by inches repeatedly) could routinely hit a very small nail with a hammer when asked. As it turned out, their hand-eye coordination was just fine thank you very much. In fact, MINUS the presence of a golf ball, these students exhibited an excellent ability to hit a marked spot on the ground with their clubhead when practice swinging. But often, once the ball was placed on that mark, they would again miss by inches (behind the ball). Why? Because no matter how much they may have understood the concept of hitting down on a conscious level, there was still a latent, intuitive desire to get below the ball and hit up at it.

This situation was not going to change until the subconscious was also convinced that hitting down would make the ball rise, and thus would release the muscles to perform anew task. As much as we may believe on a conscious level that hitting down creates good golf shots, we must convince the subconscious and our muscles as well.

Our greatest aid in this endeavour will be a successful result. Yet we won't get the successful result unless we hit down! The proverbial catch-22. Your best opportunity to convince the subconscious (and thus the muscles) to at least try to hit down is in practice, where mistakes are not penalized.

The overriding factor that that might prevent you from hitting down is fear that it will lead to a mistake that will ruin your shot (and your hole, and your game, and your day). If you take the attitude that this is just a practice session (during which you are *allowed* to make mistakes that will not impact upon your day) and that you are trying to accomplish a "task" as opposed to hitting a golf shot, then your mind will be much more willing to take "chances".

See how many times you can execute the task (striking down at the golf ball, trying to drive it DOWN into the ground) irrespective of the results. Letting go of your fear of hitting a bad shot will release the muscles to perform the desired task. Performing the task (hitting down, striking the ball and then the ground) WILL lead to good results.

We only need a few successful shots for the mind to begin to associate the positive result with the task performed. Then we might hear the mind saying in a quiet voice, "Hmmmm. Okay. That was good. I'll let you try that again." Once you are allowed to try it again, and again achieve positive results, you are on your way to practice sessions wherein you can repeatedly perform the muscular move of striking down, and simultaneously begin the task of reprogramming muscle memory.

7.6 My Shots Are Inconsistent

Sometimes there's nothing worse than hitting a good shot. "Oh right," you're saying to yourself, "and why did I buy this book?" But consider...your last six shots were a mix of fat chunkers and skinny worm burners. Suddenly -seemingly out of nowhere -"wham!" - the shot of the century. And as the ball sails toward its target,  rather than admire it in all its beauty you drop your club to the ground, your head shakes, and exasperated you ask yourself, "Why can't I do that all the time?"

Sometimes, just sometimes, doing something well occasionally is more annoying than not at all. When we seemingly fail constantly there is an underlying belief that one day we will succeed. And once we succeed, continued success will be constant; so mere sporadic success does not seem to satisfy. One of the reasons that the game of golf is so humbling is because success is no guarantee of continued success. Or so it would seem. A great shot can be followed by a lousy shot. A great round can be followed by a lousy round. And on the surface, it don't make no sense! No sense at all!

It is important to know that if your shots are inconsistent, this is an indication of a fairly significant flaw in your swing that occasionally good timing can make up for. For instance, if you are hitting up at the golf ball the overwhelming odds are that you will hit the ground before the ball (bad shot). Or, in avoiding the ground, you will skull the ball or hit it very thin(also bad shots). However, occasionally you will succeed at contacting the bottom half of the golf ball with an upswing without hitting the ground first. This is simply rolling the dice and coming up sixes. In ten attempts to hit up at the golf ball you may achieve clean contact once or twice. If your timing is really on and the lie good, maybe three or four times. If you shoot around 100 (with say, 40 putts) this may mean as many as two dozen seemingly good shots. This can drive you crazy- two dozen good shots, yet three dozen bad shots! And the bad shots aren't even predictable... some thin, some fat, some left and some right.

What is so misleading about these kinds of results is you will go away thinking you must be doing something right, and perhaps you just need more practice. But if you continue to roll the dice with your golf swing, you will have a seemingly good day once in a while (even in Vegas you win once in a while) but you will never significantly improve - no matter how much you practice. That is the cold hard truth of it. If you want to increase your odds you have to improve your golf swing, and that begins with hitting down.

7.7 I Hit My Short Irons Fine, But... It's My Long Irons & Woods I Have Difficulty With

Golf instructors hear this complaint a lot. Sad to say, rarely is it an accurate assessment of the student's game. This complaint is most often followed by, "Can you teach me how to hit my long irons (or woods)?".

Figure 39   Long irons... you must hit down to get them in the air.   Same swing, different trajectory.

Frankly, what must not happen is the appeasement of the student by attempting to teach him or her how to hit their long clubs, as that in itself implies the long clubs are swung differently. They are not.

Generally, when I'm told a student hits well with his/her short irons but poorly with their longer clubs, I ask to see them hit their short irons as I put their swings on video. Following that I will ask to record their long irons (and/or woods). In almost every case there will be little to no difference between their swing with the short irons versus that of the long. The deception lies in the result. It is said that short irons are easier to hit - and there is definite truth to that. But what also happens with a shorter iron is the ramifications of an error are more subtle.

Consider a nine iron approach to a green, say from 120

yards out. You swing, hit, and the ball misses the green just slightly to the right. What is your assessment of the result? Not that bad. So you missed the green - not the end of the world. Chip and a putt, right? And you are right, but - consider the ramifications of the SAME error that caused your miss to the right, but coming off the face of your driver, or three-iron. Picture the path the nine-iron shot was on, and imagine it on that same path for another 80 - 100 yards. Now perhaps add a pronounced slice to that path. Where do you picture the ball? Trees? Pond? Out of bounds? You see where I'm going? More importantly, do you see where the ball is going?

Simply put, if your long clubs are not performing properly it is not because you do not know how to hit long clubs, but rather it is due to an error in your swing that may or may not be obviously apparent when you hit your short irons. That error probably exists in your short irons as well, but the results are not as seemingly dramatic, giving you the perception that your swing is better with the short clubs. Make an error in your car in your local mall's parking lot and you may end up with a fender bender. No big deal. Make the same error on the freeway, at 100 km/hour? Big deal. Big deal.

So, we look at the swing on video - takeaway, swing plane, swing path (both short and long clubs), and again, in the vast majority of cases the culprit is an attempt to hit up at the ball- an action that produces more drastic results as the club gets longer. Added to this is the perception that it is more difficult to get the ball in the air with a long club and so we try even harder to hit up, only to compound the problem.

The way to hit long clubs well is to develop a good golf swing. Not a different one. And it is easier to develop a good golf swing by repeatedly swinging short irons correctly. However, as the results of your short irons can be deceiving it may be necessary to have a good instructor look at your swing. Demand that he or she be honest with you and assess accurately whether you are achieving the positions you need to hit any golf club well. As you learn the fundamentals of the golf swing yourself, you should soon be able to assess your own swing assuming that you have the benefit of a video recording of it (and the capability of slow motion and stop frame).

Now, I said that in the majority of cases involving the above scenario the swing is the same from short iron to long club. But what about the cases where it is not, you may ask? There is a human component that comes into play when we start to swing our long clubs. Greed for distance. It's quite natural. If you have selected a long club it is probably for an obvious reason - a need for distance. When you select a 9-iron you are doing so more because you need to go a *specific* distance as opposed to a lot of distance. Chances are, if it is your second shot from the fairway on a par five - or your first shot from the tee - you are looking for infinite distance. The mindset is different. If you typically hit your 3-iron 170 yards and suddenly you hit it 190, you're elated. If you typically hit your 9-iron 110 yards and suddenly you hit it 130, you ain't elated. Not as you watch it sail 20 yards over the green. Therefore, if it is revealed that you are truly hitting your short irons well yet struggling with your long clubs, the chances are you are treating your long irons differently.

It is worth repeating, the swing with a long club is the same. The fact that the club is longer and the loft is less is all that is required to hit the ball further. You do not need to swing harder. You do not need to "assist" the ball into the air (i.e. "hit up"). Remember, long clubs are supposed to hit the ball lower. And if you are getting no height at all, you are not hitting down. Go back to the beginning and start re-reading!

7.8 I Can Hit My Irons Off The Fairway, But Not My Woods

If you can hit a 3-iron off the fairway but not a fairway

wood, it stands to reason that you are treating your fairway woods differently. You needn't. You may have been told you need a flatter swing with a fairway wood. You may have been told to "sweep" the ball off the fairway with your woods. First, the very structure of the fairway wood (length of shaft, lie angle) provides a flatter swing without you having to change yours. To flatten your swing further would simply be overdoing it. It would create such a flat swing that the clubhead would come too far from the inside, leading with the heel (or worse, hosel) and send the ball dead right. Or, in a desperate last second attempt to square the clubface you would actually snap it shut and hook the ball. As for the notion of sweeping the ball, well... curlers sweep. Caretakers sweep. Golfers hit down.

Again, by virtue of the construction of your fairway wood, your angle of attack will not be as steep as shorter clubs, lessening the divot-creating action of your strike down at the ball. Of course too, the fairway wood has a bigger, specially designed sole that will prevent the club from "digging in" the way an iron does when contacting the turf. This has all been designed so that you can properly hit down at the golf ball. A "sweeping" action is an open invitation to hit up, creating a very low ball flight and shots that will predominantly go to the right.

Chapter 8

Hitting Down & the Short Game

 As much as Hit Down Dammit! is dedicated to instilling in you the need to hit down at the golf ball to hit good full golf shots, don't be surprised if it is your short game that sees the greatest improvement from learning to hit down...

8.1 Chip Shots Do Not Have To Go High

For some reason, whether it is due to the high loft of shorter clubs or the nature of the shots that make it to the highlight reels on TV, most of us get it in our heads that chip shots are supposed to fly high. However, thanks to this perception, rather than see our high-flying chips land like a butterfly, they tend to sting like a bee. High lofting short shots make it to television's highlight reels for a reason, because they are the exception and not the rule. Once we understand a basic strategy to chipping the task becomes much easier.

Almost no two chip shots are alike. Variables in chipping include the lie, the length of the grass, our distance to the edge of the green, the distance from the edge of the green to the hole, the overall distance from the ball to the hole, and the slope of the green. With all that is inconsistent in the face four chip shot, we need a constant - something from which we can base decisions on how we are going to execute the shot. We need to create a rule that we will consult, follow - or even disregard when warranted - on each shot. The rule that we shall follow is one that eliminates the guess work in one key area: where to land the ball.

Stop to consider, in the past, your thought process as to where you wanted to land the ball on a chip shot. Chances are you either never gave it a thought, or it has purely been a guessing process based on where the pin was, the slope of the green, perhaps what you had for breakfast. Let's now say that from here on in you will no longer guess where to land the ball. Something just got a whole lot easier. In order to bring consistency to your chipping you will find adopting the strategy of landing the ball at the front of the green and letting it roll to the hole will be a significant milestone.

You can have ten different chip shots that are each, say, 25 feet from ball to hole, yet each is drastically different. One may be five feet to the green and 20 more to the hole. Another may be 20 feet to the green and just 5 to the hole. And of course there are all the variations in between. Some may be uphill, while others downhill. Some over long rough, or tightly cut fairway. And let's talk about sand! But in each case there will be one thing we can count on. The front of the green. It will always be there.

Assuming you are aiming to land the ball at the front of the green, you can begin to picture the shape of the shot that will be required to:

   a) get you to the front of the green; and

   b) still allow the ball to roll the rest of the way
               to the hole.

In the case where you have 20 feet to the front of the green and only another 5 to the hole, you will want a higher lofted shot that will keep the ball in the air until it reaches its landing area, and yet not roll terribly far. In our opposite case of 5 to the green and 20 to the hole it suddenly becomes apparent that a high shot is no longer necessary. Picture a ball flight that will carry 5 feet in the air, yet land at an angle that will lead to 20 feet of roll. The two scenarios will require completely different ball flights, the same swing technique, and different clubs with which to execute the shot.

You have up to (a maximum of) fourteen clubs in your golf bag. Use them. Don't cripple your short game by limiting yourself to just one or two clubs. The typical scenario I see has a player confining himself to the use of wedge-only when chipping. They are simply asking too much of one club for a shot that we have already established is as diverse as the people the game attracts. Limiting yourself to the wedge (or any one or two clubs for that matter) puts you in a situation of having to guess where to land the ball in order for it to get to, or remain near, the hole in every situation you encounter.

Let's go back to the 5 feet to the green yet 20 to the hole situation. Hitting a pitching wedge 5 feet is no chore, but will it then roll 20? Not likely. Hit it ten and roll 15? Mmmmmaybe. But probably not. How about hit it 15 and hope it rolls 10? Perhaps. But 15 is a lot further away than 5 was, so harder to hit accurately. What if I aim for 15 but hit it twenty? Not only have I gone 5 feet too far, but it will roll more too, leaving me a long putt. If it doesn't roll into the bunker, of course.

On the other hand, we could just try our eight iron, chip it five feet, and let the ball roll the rest of the way. I'm not trying to make this sound easier than it is. There is no hard and fast rule as to what club to use, only a rule that says we have the freedom to choose. Picture the shot. Picture the ball flying in the air as high as it needs in order to reach the front of the green. Then picture it rolling like a putt to the hole. Now picture what club might create such a shot. Chances are you can reasonably narrow it down to a couple of clubs, and neither one is going to be terribly far off. Which two clubs? Only practice will tell. How high and hard you chip an eight iron, versus me or your neighbour down the street, varies.

8.11 Same Target Different Club Drill

This is one of my favourite drills because it reminds me

Figure 40   The differences in loft are just as helpful in chipping as in full shots.

of Mexico. The logic ends there. Simply, I was once on vacation in Mexico and decided to spend a leisurely morning in the sun by the chipping green. I wanted to test a theory. I spent one hour in the same spot chipping to the same hole with my wedge, determined to see how often I could get it close, and how close. In one hour, no matter what your strategy, you should have the speed and the break figured out to the point your results should be getting pretty darned good. At the end of the hour I switched clubs... to an eight iron. In five minutes my results with the eight iron were better than I'd been able to achieve in the entire hour with the wedge - including chipping in a couple of times.

This is not an "anti wedge" commercial. It is simply that for that particular shot the eight iron was a more effective choice than the wedge, no matter how many attempts I made with either club. In that particular case I was having to hit the wedge too hard to get it to the hole. As a result, where the ball landed varied, the degree of slope varied, and the roll (it tended not to roll enough) was inconsistent.

Hit Down Dammit!

Go to your local chipping green and try what I tried. Pick a spot, pick a hole, and choose two different clubs (at least 2 clubs apart e.g. wedge and 8; 9 and 7, etc.) with which to chip. Dedicate a certain amount of time to one club, then match that time with the other club, and compare the results. If you have time afterward, choose another location, a different combination of distance to green and distance to hole, and another two clubs.

8.2 The Art of Hitting Down When Chipping

Virtually everything I am about to say here will have already been said in earlier chapters. We are simply applying the same principles to chipping. What are the two most common, most annoying errors in chipping? The fat chip (chunker) that goes nowhere; and the thin chip (skull) that shoots across the green, perhaps even into the bunker the other side. Guess how they are

caused? Correct. Hitting up.

We are so determined to get the club under the ball that we either hit the ground first (and the slower clubhead speed of a chip means we cannot even muscle through the ground) and the ball goes nowhere, or, in an effort to miss the ground all together, we strike the equator (or top) of the ball with a rising leading edge, or even the sole. This leads to a low, screaming shot that goes well beyond our intended target.

If we can somehow see our way clear to striking the golf ball first, before the ground, we can achieve clean contact and dramatically improved results. The key to striking the ground after impact when chipping, is acceleration. Unfortunately, most of us are very reluctant to accelerate while executing the short game. Why? A simple fear of hitting the ball too far. We have

Hit Down Dammit!

a realistic fear of hitting this "delicate" shot way too far - past the hole, over the green, into the trap opposite perhaps. Thus, we desperately try to slow the clubhead down prior to impact. So here's the situation: not withstanding the fact we need to hit down, we have a short shot that we do not want to hit too far, yet we know we need to accelerate the clubhead in order to achieve clean contact. How do we accelerate, and yet gain control over the distance the ball will travel?

8.3 Keep the Backswing Short

The answer is simple, but not necessarily easy. Shorten your backswing. The two curses of bad chipping are trying to hit up at the ball to lift it; and swinging back too far, followed by a deceleration of the clubhead in the hopes of not hitting the ball too far. I said the answer was simple, but not easy. The trouble lies within our perception of what a short backswing equates to. We are unfortunately used to wrapping our club around our necks in an attempt to hit big booming drives so, relatively speaking, a backswing that goes to our waist seems short.

The fact is, if you were to swing back to your waist, and accelerate the clubhead down toward the ball, you would likely create a shot that travels well in excess of 25 yards. Yet here we are trying to hit a chip shot of five, ten, or fifteen yards. So, we try to – whether consciously or otherwise - s l o w the clubhead down. Decelerate. Most players I have ever taught who struggled with chipping, swung the club back not 10%, not 20 %, but 100 to 200% too far. And most were completely unaware of how far back they were swinging in the first place.

While this has been a quick tutorial in chipping, it is also vital information in understanding the connection between hitting up, and bad chipping. Hitting up at the ball will lead to bad chipping. I have found many students' poor chipping technique to be exacerbated by the fact that they were trying extra hard to hit high chip shots when they did not need to. This just led to them hitting up at the ball in an exaggerated manner which then made a bad thing worse. When you go to hit your chip high into the air, ask yourself this key question: What are you trying to get over? Unless you need to get over a bunker, a hedge, or perhaps even your ex, you would most likely be better off keeping the ball low. A ball that is low, rolls. Shots that roll are easier to predict. And, the next time they show a professional chipping in (holing out) from off the green, note whether the ball was low and rolling or high and bouncing. When a ball bounces in it does make good television, but the majority of the time you will see the ball was rolling well before it reached the hole.

8.31 Short Backswing Drill

This drill will teach you to shorten your backswing, and accelerate the clubhead. Most importantly, it will give you an awareness of how far you are swinging back, and how little backswing is actually required to hit effective shots of any nature.

> WARNING: Be prepared to be surprised,
> and frustrated. It is part of the process.

Set up on your friendly neighbourhood chipping green with a couple of dozen golf balls. Place an object such as your golf bag, or a shaft in the ground, approximately two feet behind the ball you are going to chip. Before even attempting to chip, take a few practice swings and see if you can avoid hitting the object behind you with your backswing. What seems simple, may be surprisingly difficult to do. We are just so accustomed to big backswings that the seemingly simple task of abbreviating your chipping backswing may be frustratingly difficult. There is something in our subconscious that screams out, "This is not enough! I can't hit from here!"

You can.

And you will. For one, remind yourself that this is a drill. You will *not* be penalized for poor shots. Rather than score, as would be the case out on the golf course, your focus here should be to prove (or disprove if you dare) the theory that a relatively tiny backswing will be amply sufficient to hit clean, crisp chip shots that travel the required distance.

*Figure(s)   41   Short
backswing,   accelerate
down and through.*

As you get more and more comfortable with executing the shorter backswing, you will notice how your attitude toward striking the ball will change. As opposed to in the past, where you were trying to slow the clubhead down in order to hit a shorter shot, you will now find a need, better yet *desire*, to accelerate the clubhead to make up for what will seem to be an incredibly short backswing. (On video, your backswing will look the same as those we see on TV each weekend playing the pro tours for big money). You will also find that from this shorter position, hitting down is not such a daunting task.

Thanks to centripetal force (a result of the clubhead now accelerating) you can hit down at the ball, striking the ball first, then the ground, carrying through toward your target. A decelerating clubhead lacks sufficient centripetal force for it to hold its line, and when it does strike the ground it will tend to stop right there, in the ground.

There is possibly no area of the golf game that demands
the need to hit down more than
the bunker shot. We all know
that this shot, unlike almost all
others, actually requires us to hit
behind the ball. Anywhere from
one to two inches behind it.
However, what we cannot do is
then attempt to come up at the
ball. The action must continue
downwards, full speed, through the sand.

Any attempt to come up at the ball will either see the
clubhead imbed in the sand, or - perhaps worse- miss
the sand and skull the ball into the lip of the trap or
miles over the green. We must choose a spot - one to
two inches behind the ball - and hit down at that spot
as if it were the ball. What will happen is the clubhead
will hit the sand, and the sand that is displaced as a
result will literally move the ball up and out of the
bunker. The clubhead continues down and through,
crossing the target line - not lifting - as outlined in our
earlier chapters.

There is no way to get "under the ball" in a sand trap
and it quickly becomes clear why so many who hit up
have such great difficulty with bunker shots.

Wrap Up

So that is *Hit Down Dammit!* The very fact we have been able to relate hitting down to so many areas of the game - consistency, distance, weight shift, extension, size of swing, clubhead speed, chipping, bunker play and so on - is a testament to the fact that hitting down is the most important lesson in golf.

To me, teaching you how to play golf and not teaching you how to hit down is like teaching someone how to drive a car, but never telling them how to unlock the car door. Take this lesson seriously. As I stated at the beginning, this is not a new way to play golf, it is the way. I did not make it up, I am just the guy explaining it. Hitting down is not a "system", it is just a physical fact in golf.

I cannot emphasize enough: do the drills. Never stop doing the drills. Drills are not designed to be "tried", they are designed to be repeated - indefinitely. Tour Pros do drills. Perhaps that is why they are as good as they are.

Learn to hit down at the driving range. That is the only place your mind will allow you to try something new. Try it often enough, and you will discover the results. Then let the results motivate you to practice hitting down even more.

Needless to say, seeing is believing. If you have enjoyed the theory of Hit Down Dammit! you may well benefit from the DVD series. The DVDs branch out from this book, with the main DVD *"Hit Down Dammit!"* teaching the hit down lesson. We have taken the "drills" and the "short game" components from this book and created two separate DVDs:

"Hit Down Drills"
and
"Hitting Down and the Short Game".

Then, because the success of this book created such a huge audience, much of that audience started contacting us with questions about the basic fundamentals of the golf swing. So, when we went to shoot the DVDs at beautiful Glen Abbey Golf Club, we created a fourth DVD addressing those fundamental issues, appropriately called:

"Hit Down Fun-dam-entals".

For more information about this informative DVD series visit our website at www.hitdowndammit.com.

Finally, your feedback is welcome. We welcome both your testimonials, and your questions at our website: www.hitdowndammit.com . Visit the site regularly, for updates and other golf information including the dates of Hit Down Dammit! Golf Camps that may be coming to a city near you!

It's been a pleasure passing on this vital golf swing information to you. See you on the links, and remember to *Hit Down Dammit!*

Clive Scarff

Also by Clive Scarff

Why You Suck at Golf

Do you suck at golf? Know someone who does? This book contains over 50 practical tips to fix mistakes the average amateur golfer makes regularly. A useful and fun read.

Available as a book or ebook at **hitdowndammit.com**, **amazon.com**, and other leading retailers.

Swing Issues

A collection of tips and answers to readers' questions on the golf swing. Available at **hitdowndammit.com**, **amazon.com**, and other leading ebook retailers.

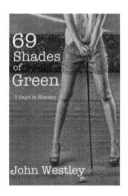

New from Thornhill Press:
69 Shades of Green

Pro golfer Dan Green rolls into Heaven, BC, ready to test his re-built swing at the Husky Open. Sparks fly when he meets Melissa – a woman of beauty, charm, & seduction and more than her fair share of skeletons. Available at **amazon.com**, and other leading ebook retailers.

Made in the USA
Middletown, DE
07 April 2016